CYBER SECURITY

The Beginners Guide to Learning
The Basics of Information Security and
Modern Cyber Threats

By:

Noah Zhang

Published By:

Dana Publishing
P.O. Box 1801
Mentor, OH 44060

Legal & Disclaimer

Table of Contents

Introduction to Cyber Security

The term Cyber Security is a broad-based terminology for Information Security

This guide is for anyone that wants to increase their awareness of securing their digital activities and anyone getting started in the cyber security field.

The objective of this book is to point out the potential areas of weakness in facilities and as an individual, and give basic frameworks and defense strategies which would significantly reduce the chances of being infiltrated. This includes establishing a risk management framework, which entails integrating cyber risk into the firm problems and making it a managerial priority. The company is meant to adapt cyber risk into its risk mitigation and defense strategies; this will be molded into its organizational behavior and become part of the process.

The book also addresses things such as basic operations risks, which deal with companies or individuals. We will look at the basics of network defense, enforcement of access control, logging, and monitoring for more secure activities.

The book also points out people as essential risks to any enterprise or network (Even home networks). Cyber weakness is tricky considering it can happen at any time or place. People need to be made aware of the potential danger they pose to the security systems of a company. This orientation, as well as stricter policies for access control and authentication, should help to mitigate this issue in the long run.

As such, a cybersecurity problem should not be treated as an 'if in this current world, but in terms of 'when' it is going to happen, and so this book is here to help with the preparation for these scenarios for a non-technical person or beginner in information security. This includes management systems, IT auditing, and best practice policies. Exemplary cybersecurity readiness involves an understanding of the threats to assets and the information that is relevant to the company, not to mention its people—while monitoring and detecting cybersecurity threats regularly.

When a breach happens, the faster it is detected and responded to—the better the chances of reducing the overall loss. The question then is how fast the company is able to respond and identify the theft of the information or disable the main services? How easily can the corrupted information be verified and can be made ready for access, along with the details of the incident response plan? There is also a need to preserve and analyze the logs, as it can assist in showing how the attack happened and how that leak can be sealed. It is not just enough to plug the hole but to also safeguard it against future attacks. The key is to be preventive and creative, rather than reactive to such attacks. These are all factors that need to be considered in the event of infiltration, but not all corporations have such protocols. We will also briefly discuss career opportunities and which ones may keep growing exponentially and which ones may fall by the wayside as a result of automation or (A.I.).

Chapter 1: The State of Cyber Security

Cyber threats come in many guises, from personal identity theft to corporate hijacking to institutional/national security hacks. As technology advances, it seems that the ranks of invaders—even computer terrorists— grow just as quickly.

Basically, these threats break down into three categories:

Attacks on confidentiality: Credit card fraud is rampart in our world, as is identity theft. Both are criminal acts and inherent invasions of privacy; personal information is released to a potentially ever larger group of hackers, the person who was attacked must rectify the situation to great inconvenience. On a more public, more dangerous level are spies who focus on nations or states. Their activities focus on obtaining confidential data for military, economic or political gain.

Attacks on integrity: Integrity attacks, or sabotage, aim to damage or obliterate systems or information and those who use and rely on them. They can be as subtle as a typo or as blatant as an out-and-out smear campaign aimed to destroy the target.

Attacks on availability: The use of ransomware or "denial-of-service" are attacks on availability. The ransom comes into play when a price is demanded to decrypt the target's data, while denial-of-service swamps a network resource with requests, making the service unavailable.

More specifically, here are some ways that these attacks are carried out.

A backdoor, also known as a cryptosystem or algorithm, is a

way to bypass normal security controls such as passwords. They can be authorized (as for a specific purpose) or added by an attacker. In any case, they create a vulnerability. With the goal of making a computer or resource unavailable, denial-of-service attacks can occur when incorrect passwords are entered multiple times, thus locking the account, or by overloading the system with requests and blocking all users. These attacks can stem from zombie computers or even from duping innocent systems into sending unwanted traffic.

Eavesdropping is exactly what it sounds like—listening to private communications between network hosts. Certain programs are used by government agencies to "audit" ISPs. This widespread practice extends to closed systems when electro-magnetic transmissions are monitored.

Masquerading through falsifying data in order to gain access to unauthorized data is called spoofing and comes in many forms: email spoofing, forgery of a sending address; MAC spoofing, changing the Media Access Control address to pose as a valid user; biometric spoofing, faking a biometric sample; IP address spoofing, altering the source IP address to hide identity or impersonate another system.

Through physical access or direct-access attacks, a perpetrator can copy data, compromise security, install listening devices or worms and more. Even protected systems are vulnerable to this type of attack.

Phishing frequently uses email spoofing or instant messaging to direct a user to enter confidential information by looking almost the same as the legitimate site.

Through privilege escalation, an attacker can escalate their access level by fooling the system into granting access to restricted data or resources.

Clickjacking is literally hijacking a user to click on a link or icon to another website other than the intended one. Particularly sneaky, clickjacking routes the clicks, or sometimes keystrokes, to an irrelevant page.

By impersonating an institution, bank, customer or other entity, social engineering leads users to reveal passwords, credit card numbers and other private information. This scam reportedly costs U.S. businesses more than $2 billion every two years.

Without computers, the world would slip back into pre-Industrial Revolution mode. Technology has streamlined every aspect of life, particularly for businesses and other public entities, some of which are more and more at risk.

Financial systems: Financial regulators, investment banks and commercial banks attract cybercriminals who see an avenue to market manipulation and illegal gains. Any website than enables transfer of funds or buying goods is also a target, as are ATMs, which are frequently hacked for customer data and PINs.

Utilities and Industry: Vital services including the power grid, nuclear power plants, water and gas networks and telecommunications are controlled by computers. It has been proven that even those controlled by computers not connected to the Internet (Air Gaps) are vulnerable to attack as well. Once again, social engineering and human errors are responsible for a large part of intrusions, hacks and breaches today.

Aviation: One power outage at a major airport can have a tumultuous ripple effect on air traffic. Radio transmissions would be disrupted, an in-plane attack can occur, loss of system integrity and aircraft, and air traffic control outages are just some of the possible outcomes.

Personal devices: All of those wonderful gadgets that people use to simplify life—smart phones, tablets, smart watches, activity trackers—can be exploited through built-in cameras and other devices. Attackers can collect health other personal information or use the device networks as paths to an attack.

Corporations: Identity theft and data breaches such as credit card information have been aimed at large corporations such as Target Corporation and Equifax. In some cases, foreign governments attempt to spread propaganda or spy through attacks. Health insurance fraud, which costs everyone, and impersonation of patients to obtain drugs for illicit purposes, are also common. Despite these activities, 62% of all organizations did not augment security training in 2015.

Autos: Today's vehicles practically drive themselves, and the day when this common is not far off. Cruise control, airbags, anti-lock brakes and other features make driving more enjoyable and, hopefully, safer. WIFI and Bluetooth keep the cars connected and raise the possibility of security breaches.

Government: Attacks on government and military systems create chaos, disrupt services and—to the extreme—qualify as acts of terrorism. Whether it is an activist, foreign government or other hackers, the result is infrastructure malfunction of personnel records, police and other first responder communications, student records, traffic controls and financial systems. Widespread computerization of personal identity items such as passports and access cards also lead to vulnerability in this area.

Internet of things (IoT): Physical objects that carry sensors, software or any type of network connection to store and share data are part of the Internet of things. A building, vehicle or appliance can comprise the IoT, and the proliferation of this modern phenomenon creates the possibility for physical—not just virtual—threat. For instance, a stolen cellphone can unlock a residence or hotel room door. IoT is also prevalent in the industrial markets now, known as IIoT.

Medical systems: Viruses, breaches of sensitive medical data, diagnostic equipment, and other devices are potential targets of attacks. These threats are deemed so likely that, in 2016, the U.S. Food and Drug Administration created guidelines for secure maintenance of manufacturers of medical devices. However, no recommendations or structure for implementation were included.

A syntactic attack comes after your network through different channels. These attacks are often carried out through malicious programs. The most common programs used for syntactic attacks are as detailed below.

Trojan horses - A trojan horse is something that looks harmless. You will allow it into your system, unaware of the danger it possesses. Today, trojan horses can be sent using several methods, including hackers cloning an email. The email will look like it comes from someone you know or trust, but its main purpose is to steal your information or destroy your system - whichever reason the hackers sent it.

Worms - Worms are unique. They do not need the action of another program to spread through your computer or network. Worms are often deployed as secret agents. They collect and report information about your network to the hackers. They spread very fast in a network and can cripple it as soon as the hacker accomplishes their goals.

Viruses - A virus is basically a program that is attached to another program or file. They replicate when you access the infected program or file. Viruses are common in shared and downloaded files and attachments sent through email. When the virus is activated, it can send itself to every person on your contact list.

Securing a Wireless Network

It is crucial for people to learn how to protect their wireless networks to ensure their confidential information does not fall into the wrong hands. This chapter will give a brief introduction to securing a personal wireless network and how to do it. For most of the examples, NETGEAR routers will be used. If users have a different router, keep in mind that some things will be different.

Encryption

Let us begin by discussing basic encryption. Encryption, when regarding data movement over a network, is the process by which plaintext is converted into a scrambled mixture of characters. This decreases the probability that the information that was sent over an encrypted network is being used for malicious purposes. As for encryption regarding wireless routers, it is the process by which an encrypted authentication key is produced every time the correct login credentials are entered, allowing access to the network. In simpler terms, every time a user logs in to a secured router, a unique key is generated which allows access to that internet connection.

WPA

WiFi Protected Access or WPA is a security tool that was developed to replace WEP security. There are two types: WPA and WPA2. The difference is that WPA2 is a newer, more secure version of WPA. Anytime users have to log in to a wireless network, whether it's at their house or at school, they are most likely, logging into a WPA/WPA2 encrypted network. These security features work by checking whether or not the login credentials entered are accurate (The PSK or pre-shared key), and if they are, an encrypted authentication key unique to that very login is generated. Once this key is generated, it is checked by the corresponding network, allowing the transmission of data to start, assuming the login credentials were a match. Now that we have seen the basics of WPA encryption, we will discuss some basic steps that can be taken to secure personal wireless networks.

Wireless router credentials

When a wireless router is first set up, it is very important that the default login credentials are changed. Most personal wireless routers come with a standard login username and password such as:

- Username: **admin**

- Password: **password**

Hackers know these default login credentials by vendor or MAC address, all of which is sent out in the clear when your wireless card is on; thus, it is crucial that they are changed right away. Using a lengthy password with a combination of characters, both upper and lower case will give users reliably secure credentials.

Service Set Identifier

A Service Set Identifier (SSID) refers to the computer language for the name of a wireless network. For example, the University of Arizona's wireless network is known as 'UAWifi.' It is important to change the name of a personal network from the default, as hackers may target a wireless network with a default name, thinking it is less secure. To further improve security, SSID broadcasting can be turned off. This means that the network will not be visible to outsiders. It will still be there, and if the specific SSID is searched for, it can be found. However, anyone scanning for a network to connect to won't be able to see this hidden network. This is especially useful when you have neighbors who are trying to gain access to your personal network.

Media Access Control

Media Access Control (MAC) is a set of numbers used to identify a specific device. Every device, whether it's a computer, tablet, or phone has a unique MAC address. To better protect a network, the router can be set to only allow specific MAC addresses to connect to that network. This adds another layer of security to your network by only permitting specific devices to connect. While this is a useful security feature, it is important to at least mention that there are software programs available that allow hackers to fake MAC addresses, allowing them to pretend to be the same device that's on your network.

The last tip we have for securing a router is the most effective method of keeping personal networks secure, turn the router off. If you're going on vacation or you simply won't be using their network for an extended period, turning off the router is the best way to avoid hackers from getting into the network. They cannot access something that is not powered on and transmitting data.

Chapter 2: Threat Landscape

Cyber threats come in many guises, from personal identity theft to corporate hijacking to institutional/national security hacks. As technology advances, it seems that the ranks of invaders—even computer terrorists— grow just as quickly.

Basically, these threats break down into three categories.

Attacks on confidentiality: Credit card fraud is rampart in our world, as is identity theft. Both are criminal acts and inherent invasions of privacy; personal information is released to a potentially ever larger group of hackers, the person who was attacked must rectify the situation to great inconvenience. On a more public, more dangerous level are spies who focus on nations or states. Their activities focus on obtaining confidential data for military, economic or political gain.

Attacks on integrity: Integrity attacks, or sabotage, aim to damage or obliterate systems or information and those who use and rely on them. They can be as subtle as a typo or as blatant as an out-and-out smear campaign aimed to destroy the target.

Attacks on availability: The use of ransomware or denial-of-service are attacks on availability. The ransom comes into play when a price is demanded to decrypt the target's data, while denial-of-service swamps a network resource with requests, making the service unavailable.

More specifically, here are some ways that these attacks are carried out.

- A backdoor, also known as a cryptosystem or algorithm, is a way to bypass normal security controls such as passwords. They can be authorized (as for a specific purpose) or added by an attacker. In any case, they create a vulnerability.

- With the goal of making a computer or resource unavailable, denial-of-service attacks can occur when incorrect passwords are entered multiple times, thus locking the account, or by overloading the system with requests and blocking all users. These attacks can stem from zombie computers or even from duping innocent systems into sending unwanted traffic.

- Eavesdropping is exactly what it sounds like—listening to private communications between network hosts. Certain programs are used by government agencies to "audit" ISPs. This widespread practice extends to closed systems when electro-magnetic transmissions are monitored.

- Masquerading through falsifying data in order to gain access to unauthorized data is called spoofing and comes in many forms: email spoofing, forgery of a sending address; MAC spoofing, changing the Media Access Control address to pose as a valid user; biometric spoofing, faking a biometric sample; IP address spoofing, altering the source IP address to hide identity or impersonate another system.

- Through physical access or direct-access attacks, a perpetrator can copy data, compromise security, install listening devices or worms and more. Even protected systems are vulnerable to this type of attack.

- Phishing frequently uses email spoofing or instant messaging to direct a user to enter confidential information by looking almost the same as the legitimate site.

- Through privilege escalation, an attacker can escalate their access level by fooling the system into granting access to restricted data or resources.

- Clickjacking is literally hijacking a user to click on a link or icon to another website other than the intended one. Particularly sneaky, clickjacking routes the clicks, or sometimes keystrokes, to an irrelevant page.

- By impersonating an institution, bank, customer or other entity, social engineering leads users to reveal passwords, credit card numbers and other private information. This scam reportedly costs U.S. businesses more than $2 billion every two years.

Without computers, the world would slip back into pre-Industrial Revolution mode. Technology has streamlined every aspect of life, particularly for businesses and other public entities, some of which are more and more at risk.

Financial systems: Financial regulators, investment banks and commercial banks attract cybercriminals who see an avenue to market manipulation and illegal gains. Any website than enables transfer of funds or buying goods is also a target, as are ATMs, which are frequently hacked for customer data and PINs.

Utilities and Industry: Vital services including the power grid, nuclear power plants, water and gas networks and telecommunications are controlled by computers. It has been proven that even those controlled by computers not connected to the Internet are vulnerable to attack.

Aviation: One power outage at a major airport can have a tumultuous ripple effect on air traffic. Radio transmissions would be disrupted, an in-plane attack can occur, loss of system integrity and aircraft, and air traffic control outages are just some of the possible outcomes.

Personal devices: All of those wonderful gadgets that people use to simplify life—smart phones, tablets, smart watches, activity trackers—can be exploited through built-in cameras and other devices. Attackers can collect health other personal information or use the device networks as paths to an attack.

Corporations: Identity theft and data breaches such as credit card information have been aimed at large corporations such as Target Corporation and Equifax. In some cases, foreign governments attempt to spread propaganda or spy through attacks. Health insurance fraud, which costs everyone, and impersonation of patients to obtain drugs for illicit purposes, are also common. Despite these activities, 62% of all organizations did not augment security training in 2015.

Autos: Today's vehicles practically drive themselves, and the day when this common is not far off. Cruise control, airbags, anti-lock brakes and other features make driving more enjoyable and, hopefully, safer. WIFI and Bluetooth keep the cars connected and raise the possibility of security breaches.

Government: Attacks on government and military systems create chaos, disrupt services and—to the extreme—qualify as acts of terrorism. Whether it is an activist, foreign government or other hackers, the result is infrastructure malfunction of personnel records, police and other first responder communications, student records, traffic controls and financial systems. Widespread computerization of personal identity items such as passports and access cards also lead to vulnerability in this area.

Internet of things (IoT): Physical objects that carry sensors, software or any type of network connection to store and share data are part of the Internet of things. A building, vehicle or appliance can comprise the IoT, and the proliferation of this modern phenomenon creates the possibility for physical—not just virtual—threat. For instance, a stolen cellphone can unlock a residence or hotel room door.

Medical systems: Viruses, breaches of sensitive medical data, diagnostic equipment, and other devices are potential targets of attacks. These threats are deemed so likely that, in 2016, the U.S. Food and Drug Administration created guidelines for secure maintenance of manufacturers of medical devices. However, no recommendations or structure for implementation were included.

Chapter 3: Data Encryption

Data encryption is the process where data is translated into a different code or form, such that the only people who can access and read it are those who have a decryption key, which is also referred to as a secret key. Encrypted data is also known as ciphertext. Unencrypted data is referred to as plaintext. Considering the security threats in the global environment, encryption is one of the best policies businesses, organizations, governments, and individuals are using to protect their data.

Cryptography in Information Security

Information is one of the most valuable assets in any organization. Efforts towards system protection are geared towards three results: confidentiality, integrity, and availability of data. However much someone might try to make you believe it, no security control is 100 percent effective. Encryption is the last prevention mechanism that is often implemented, especially in a layered security model.

Most people hear the mention of encryption and believe they are safe already. This is another fallacy. Encryption is not the end of your troubles. Some hackers have access to very powerful computers that can decrypt any such information. Therefore, encryption is one of many procedures that you can implement to protect your interests.

Cryptography is a scientific concept where complex logic and mathematical equations are used to generate robust encryption methods. Once the meaning of the undersigned data is obfuscated, the artistic element of cryptography comes into play.

Cryptography can be traced back to Sun Tzu's art of war. Field commanders, secret agents and other relevant parties relied on information. To keep this information from falling into the wrong hands, they had to hide its meaning. This allowed them the benefit of surprise, timing, and concealed maneuver. The earliest forms of cryptography relied on codes, transposition, and substitution to conceal their messages.

The threat of cybercrime is always rising. In response, security systems must be built more sophisticated than they were before. Experts keep trying to tighten their grip on communication security in order to make sure there are no loopholes that hackers can exploit. This is done through data encryption. There are two types of data encryption: asymmetric encryption and symmetric encryption.

Asymmetric Encryption

Asymmetric encryption uses private and public keys. Both of these keys are mathematical and perform a specific role within the operation. Data that is encrypted with a public key can only be decrypted with a private key and vice versa; it is impossible to encrypt and decrypt data with the same key.

Private keys must be kept private, lest the security of the entire system is compromised. In the case that you believe the private key has been hacked or compromised in any way, you are required to generate a new one. Asymmetric encryption is considered a stronger and better option compared to symmetric encryption in terms of data protection. However, the challenge with asymmetric encryption is that it's slower than symmetric encryption. As a result, it is not the best option for bulk encryption.

In asymmetric encryption, data is transferred between two parties. Both the sender and the recipient will receive an access key set. The sender must encrypt the information with their private key before it is sent. The recipient on the other hand must use their public key to decrypt the information.

In order to efficiently use this encryption method, digital certificates are used in the client-server communication platform. This certificate holds critical information, such as the location of the user, their email address, the organization to which the certificate originated, the public key of the user, and any other information that can be used to identify the user and their server.

Whenever the server and client need to communicate over encrypted information, they must both send queries across the network, informing the other of their intentions. Once the queries are received, the recipient receives a copy of the certificate. This certificate holds the public key the recipient will need to access the encrypted information.

One of the most prominent uses of asymmetric encryption is in blockchain computing. Bitcoin especially made this form of encryption very popular, because it was used in determining proof of work in Bitcoin mining. In the Bitcoin ecosystem, the Elliptic Curve Digital Signature Algorithm (ECDSA) is used to generate private and public keys. These keys then legitimize the digital transactions involved. Through asymmetric encryption, it is very difficult for anyone to alter any information that has already been loaded onto the blockchain.

Asymmetric encryption is currently being adopted by many businesses and organizations. While it can be scaled up for different purposes, the two main reasons why companies use it are for encryption and creating digital signatures. Digital signatures authenticate data, giving validity to the communications. The recipient is confident that they are accessing information from the sender without the risk of data breach happening anywhere in between. This eliminates the risk of man-in-the-middle attacks.

Digital signatures also confer an element of finality to information shared. The sender cannot claim at a later date that they did not sign or authorize the document. Once their digital signature is appended to it, they are responsible for it.

The commonly used algorithms in asymmetric encryption are:

- RSA
- Diffie-Hellman
- DSA
- El Gamal
- ECC

As soon as the digital signature is verified, the protocol checks to ascertain whether the content is still the same as it was when the sender appended their signature. If any changes have been made to the original copy - even the slightest change - authentication will fail.

Symmetric Encryption

Symmetric encryption is considered one of the conventional encryption methods. It is most likely the easiest. The encryption is performed by using one secret key (symmetric key). Both the recipient and sender have access to the secret key, which is needed to encrypt and decrypt the information. Before the sender dispatches the message, they must encrypt it using the symmetric key. The recipient, on the other hand, must use the same key to decrypt the message.

Considering how simple the encryption and decryption process is, symmetric encryption is easy and takes a shorter time compared to asymmetric encryption. There are many modern approaches to symmetric encryption, which use unique algorithms such as the following:

- **Blowfish** - This is an algorithm that was built to replace DES. It is a symmetric cypher that splits messages into 64-bit blocks and individually encrypts each of the blocks.

- **AES** - This is a standard encryption method used by the US government and a lot of organizations. AES is very reliable in 128 bits but can also be used as 192 bits and 256 bits, especially for resource intensive encryption.

Other algorithms include:

- QUAD

- DES

- 3DES

- RC4

Even without your knowledge, you constantly use symmetric encryption to access the internet. The most common application is when the client interacts with a server that has an SSL certificate. The server and client negotiate a connection and, once approved, they exchange 256-bit session keys to allow communication over an encrypted network.

Comparing Symmetric and Asymmetric Encryption

While asymmetric encryption requires two keys, symmetric encryption only uses a single key. Therefore, symmetric encryption is a rather straightforward approach. Both of these encryption methods access data through a secret key.

While symmetric encryption has been in use for a long time, it does have challenges, especially in secure communication, which necessitates the need for organizations, entities, and individuals to adopt asymmetric encryption. The main advantage that symmetric encryption has over asymmetric encryption is that you can transfer a lot of data through it.

Asymmetric encryption was created in response to the challenge of sharing keys as we see in symmetric encryption. Therefore, with public-private keys, you no longer have to share keys to access encrypted information.

The Role of Data Encryption

There are many reasons why data encryption is an issue you should take seriously. The main reason, however, is to protect the integrity and confidentiality of the data on your computer networks and the transmission over the internet to other computer networks. Modern algorithms are in use today to protect data and replace the data encryption standard (DES), which is an outdated algorithm. Why is encryption important to your business? We have outlined some reasons below.

Protecting data handling - Encryption offers a guarantee of data security all the time. One of the most vulnerable moments in data handling is the point at which it is transferred from one place to another. This is where most hackers pounce. *Man-in-the-middle* attacks were very common in the past *(Li, 2019)*. A hacker would intercept information, tamper with it, and pass it on to the recipient. The recipient would access and use the data, believing it to be the gospel truth. Through encryption, data is protected when it is in transit or when it is in storage. It does not matter whether you feel the data is important or not, you should always make sure it is encrypted, *especially when under storage.*

Ensuring integrity - Hackers do not just want to steal your information. Once they have access to it, they can alter it in such a way that it benefits them if someone acts on it as they should have. Unknown to the user, they will be aiding the hacker's objectives. Through encryption, you can ensure the integrity of data is maintained. Skilled hackers can still make a few changes to encrypted data. However, if this happens, the data is corrupted and cannot be used for whatever purpose it was supposed to be used for. Therefore, you immediately realize you have been hacked and initiate the necessary response mechanisms. *Hashing is a great way to ensure integrity.*

The case for privacy - Encryption is important in terms of privacy protection. There is a lot of data that we share with apps, websites and companies. Some companies hold too much data about us; anyone who has access to it for criminal reasons can execute the perfect identity theft crime. From personal information to location details and credit card information, encryption ensures that this data is inaccessible to the wrong people, especially if they manage to intercept it. They cannot use the data they obtain unless they have the decryption keys.

Encryption, therefore, offers assurance to users that privacy and anonymity online can be a real thing again. Government agencies and criminals can no longer intercept and monitor your communication by doing the bare minimum. The interesting thing about encryption is that some of the protocols and technology available at the moment are too powerful, so some governments are thinking of limiting the effectiveness. This poses risks to individuals, companies, businesses, and other entities. It is almost like locking your door when you leave for work, but leaving the key under the mat.

Compliance - In light of some of the cyber security risks that companies have experienced over the years, several changes have been made, and it is important to comply lest the company is sued for not doing their best to protect the customer data in their care. The GDPR *(Smouter, 2018)*, for example, allows consumers to report any instance where they feel the companies they interact with are not handling their data in a diligent manner.

In most industries, compliance regulations are very strict. The idea here is to make sure that, other than the personal information that the companies hold, their intellectual property rights and any other data that might be privileged is protected from unauthorized access.

One of the regulations the ***Health Insurance Portability and Accountability Act*** (HIPAA) demands is that companies must go the extra mile and institute the best security protocols to protect the records of their patients, especially concerning sensitive health information *(See, 2003)*. Encryption is not just about meeting compliance requirements; it is also about protecting the valuable customer data organizations hold.

Cross-device protection - Today, we access the internet and different networks from a variety of devices. All these devices must be protected from unauthorized access. This is where encryption comes in handy. Data transfer is always the riskiest bit of handling data. You might have your company devices protected, but your home devices are not. If you attempt a data transfer on such a device, you risk exposing yourself and the company to unknown dangers. Through encryption, these devices can all be protected, such that you can store and share data across any of the devices you have access to without worrying about someone monitoring your activities or looking forward to intercept your data.

The increasing risk of hacking - Hacking is no longer the activity of a few smart kids who feel bored and have too much time on their hands; hacking is currently one of the biggest businesses in the world. In some cases, hackers operate under the protection of a foreign country. This is just how serious hackers need to get your data. In light of these challenges, encrypting your data makes it difficult for hackers to access it, and even if they do, more often than not there isn't much they can do with it.

It is important for the reader to understand that it is not always a real live person doing the hacking. Global threats are now automated by software and botnets which are controlled by command and control servers. High value targets are definitely targeted by highly skilled hacker groups or criminal organizations.

For example; take your home router, it is scanned and pinged almost non-stop every day by Internet software from various global proxy servers and machines looking for a weakness to exploit on your network. The software available today is very advanced and growing, scanning millions of IP addresses in not a big deal anymore.

Challenges in Implementing Encryption Protocols

Data protection is one of the most common discussions that is being had at the moment. It is a priority that cannot be wished away. Companies that have suffered data breaches in the past also suffered financial losses in terms of compensation packages and expensive lawsuits.

The need for encryption is driven by two factors: compliance and the need to reduce risk. To do this, there exists an elaborate path to encryption that involves classifying risks, discovery, protecting the system, enforcing encryption protocols, and evaluating/monitoring the network to make sure everything runs as it should. Encryption might have been in use for many years, but there are challenges that are unique to the process that must be considered when implementing encryption solutions. We have outlined some of these challenges below.

Performance challenges - Encryption will always add a performance overhead to your systems. The higher your need for encryption, the more you should spend on getting supercomputers that can process large transactions without straining resources. Without this, you must brace yourself for a sluggish performance for all the other systems connected to your network when you are encrypting or decrypting some data.

Managing encryption programs - You have to determine the best encryption method that's suitable for your business. However, this is not the end of your challenges. You must also think about building a plan for system integration and establishing an environment that is secure and reliable.

Are you certain your encryption programs will meet the compliances and requirements in your industry? How easy is it for you to integrate the encryption protocols in data formatting, performance testing, and setting formal policies?

Key length - The other concern that companies experience with encryption is the appropriate key length and algorithms. There are several algorithms available. Choosing the best one depends on the development environment you operate in. At the same time, the ideal encryption key should be longer to reduce the risk of easy decryption. However, at the same time, the longer the key, the heavier network resources you will have to allocate to encryption and decryption. This will definitely affect other parts of the business.

Key management - Key storage and management is the other challenge in encryption. Once you have your data encrypted, where do you store the keys? This is actually a critical discussion. You must consider this in terms of the approaches that are aligned with your business needs. Ensure you keep changing the keys regularly and never use swap keys. Keys must only be accessible on the premise.

Data discovery - How do you access the encrypted data? The business needs swift access to important data. This is a board level decision, from where the relevant stakeholders can agree on the best way and assign data custodians.

Data querying - Querying encrypted data will help with retrieval when needed. This data can be stored on the cloud or on the premise. The challenge for most organizations is that some data will be decrypted several times, especially if it is important to the daily operations of the business. This also increases the risk that hackers might intercept the decrypted data. Remember that subsequent decryption also increases the resource demands.

Encryption Mistakes That Leave You Exposed

Encryption is the subject of many discussions about cyber security today. It has helped to keep hackers at bay, but that is not the end of it. There are a few mistakes that people make that will eventually render their encryption processes useless in the face of attacks.

Think about it - if all these encryption protocols are so good, why is it that governments and businesses are constantly attacked and have loads of data stolen? Over recent years, there are many applications that have made their way into our devices. These applications demand more cryptographic procedures to protect them and support their functionalities.

One problem that these applications have is that those who use them do not use encryption protocols the way they should. As a result, the user and the applications end up with a false notion of security, which only becomes apparent the moment they are hacked. We have detailed some of the common mistakes that threaten to derail the success of encryption below.

Using low-level encryption - People are not taking encryption seriously at all. Companies are still encrypting data through file encryption or disk encryption, which are some of the lowest level encryption protocols. Did you know that disk encryption only works when your server is off? As long as your server is on, your operating system will keep decrypting your data such that anyone who has access to the network has access to the data. If there were to be a simple data breach, all of your information will be vulnerable.

Assuming you have the best security experts - One of the biggest mistakes you can make is to assume that the developers in your company are the best security experts in the industry. Your engineers might be some of the most amazing coders you will come across in your entire lifetime, but this does not make them the best in security.

It is sad, but even some of the most brilliant developers in the world come nowhere close to being the best at IT security. IT is a very wide field. It is almost impossible for one person to be experts at all aspects of IT. At the beginning of their careers, most people make the mistake of thinking they can handle anything that is thrown their way. However, once they settle into their careers, they pick a path and specialize in it.

In most cases, security experts are system administrators. Unless their job description says otherwise, you will hardly ever find them writing code. An exception is when you need them to break into some system. One of the challenges that software developers have is pride. They take pride in figuring things out and coming up with solutions to problems. It is, therefore, highly unlikely that any of them will admit that they do not know how to protect your system. In fact, most of them feel threatened and overlooked when you bring in an expert to handle the security of your system. They might even rebel.

Do not find yourself in that trap. Leave security to experts. For encryption implementation, you only have one chance, and you must get it right. If your developer makes a mistake with the code they write, you might notice an error with rendering on a specific web page. However, if this mistake is experienced in security, your entire network might be at risk. To make matters worse, you might not even realize the error in their code until it is too late.

Wrong use of algorithms and cipher modes - When encrypting personal and sensitive data, there are so many algorithms that you can use. Unfortunately, not all of them are suitable for the reasons that you use them. You must do your research to ensure the encryption algorithms applied are suitable. A lot of developers barely understand the risks they put their businesses through with such challenges.

Human interference - No matter how good encryption is, it is useless without the human interface. The weakest link is always the end user. While encryptions might be mathematically sound, their complexity can make it difficult for users to understand and implement them. As a result, some people end up disabling encryption altogether without reporting it to the necessary authorities within the organization. By the time you realize your data was never encrypted, hackers will have already done quite a number on you.

Inappropriate key management - How are you managing the encryption keys? Inappropriate management is the simplest and easiest way for your data to end up in the wrong hands. Even if you use the best encryption program, once you are careless about key management, all your efforts will be futile.

There are so many mistakes people make with encryption keys. Assuming all the information is signed and encrypted properly, some common mistakes people make include keeping the key in a configuration file within the application and storing it on the file system or somewhere within the database.

Some developers do not even protect the keys. They might find a good place to keep the keys, but still leave it vulnerable. Your encryption key is needed to decrypt information, and you should also encrypt the encryption key. This is a procedure referred to as key encryption key (KEK). The KEK should be kept in a different location from your system. It is also possible to protect the KEK with a master signing key or master encryption key. All these are important layers of protection that you should consider, but most people never do.

So, let's say you generate an encryption key that you feel is perfect for protecting your information; however, you use the same key for everything. This is no different from having 123456 as your password. If someone breaks into your system and accesses your encryption key, you can be sure they will try to use it to decrypt anything else that they come across. This lucky guess might be your downfall.

The other challenge is developers who do not plan to change the encryption key. From time to time, you must review your security apparatus and change the encryption keys. The same risk that applies when you use the same encryption key for all services applies here too. Someone will try their luck, and once they are inside your system, they can operate covertly until they achieve their mission.

Regulatory compliance does not guarantee security - The demand for compliance should not be mistaken as a security guarantee. Your networks and systems might be complaint with certain regulations, but this should not mean you lower your guard. While regulations demand that you comply to set standards, some of them barely mention how you should go about it.

In light of this challenge, it is very easy to mess up data security. Unfortunately, when things get rough, the regulations will not cover you. In fact, they will be used to crucify you. To make matters worse, a lot of developers these days add the most basic level of encryption to their code and assume that everything is perfect. This gives your business a false sense of assurance and security, until you realize later on that you were never protected in the first place.

Trusting cloud service providers - Cloud service providers are just like any other business people; they will use beautiful language to interest you in their services. The subscription business is worth billions if not trillions of dollars a year. Given that server-side applications and cloud computing are experiencing an unprecedented growth at the moment, everyone is excited about migrating their businesses to cloud storage platforms operated by giants like Google, Microsoft, and Amazon.

Sure, these service providers take the necessary precautionary measures to keep their services safe. They invest millions of dollars in cyber security to protect their customers and to position their businesses as the best cloud solutions. As a result of this, many people assume that once they create an account and transfer data to the cloud, they are safe, but this is wrong.

While the physical infrastructure that serves these cloud services might be safe, and in some cases, may even offer

34

encryption services, you must perform your own encryption services from your end. Before you move any data to the cloud, make sure it is encrypted. To be fair, data encryption is your prerogative, not the cloud service provider's. In case they offer encryption services alongside the cloud services that you are paying for, this is good for you, because you will enjoy multiple levels of encryption. If they do not, you must ensure your data is protected. Remember that ignorance is never a suitable defense.

While this discussion might paint an ugly picture of the encryption landscape, it is not all doom and gloom. There is a lot that you can do to make sure you are protected, safe, and using the right procedures to protect your data. Consult experts whenever you can.

Debunking Myths About Data Encryption

You do not need to be a cryptographic nerd to understand the concept of encryption or why it is important. It is simple, really; it is hiding your information behind code so that it is useless to anyone who accesses it without the right decryption codes. Over the years, there have been misconceptions that exist about encryption. Most of these are founded on lies or half-truths. The following is a brief assessment of these myths and logical reasons why they are not true.

Encryption Is the Preserve of Big Organizations

One of the biggest misconceptions is this one. Perhaps the origin might be traced back to the fact that, whenever encryption is discussed, the discussions center around big organizations. It is fairly easy to understand why people might think about this.

Encryption is not just for big organizations; anyone who shares information across the internet needs encryption. Today, it is not just the big organizations that are targeted by hackers, but also individuals. No one is safe. As long as you are online, know that someone is always watching.

Did you know that more than 40 percent of cyber attacks target small businesses and individuals? The reason for this is because they are notorious for having weak security systems. Therefore, the cybercriminals can easily find whatever they need from them. Without encryption, someone can hack into your devices and use them as a means of getting into another system. Your devices can be hacked on your unsecured home network, and when you connect your devices to the home network, the hacker migrates to the work network, which was their intention all along.

To prevent your data from falling into the wrong hands, try to make sure you encrypt your data. There are several ways to go about it. You can find simpler solutions for your home devices and appliances. Remember that whether you are running a small business or simply have a personal network at home, encrypting your data is important.

Bogs Down the Network

The issue of encryption and resource consumption is a fair one. Most of the time, you will suffer some sluggish performance on the network when encrypting or decrypting some data. However, you should refrain from using this as an excuse not to encrypt and protect your data. The benefits of encrypting your information outweigh the challenges involved in a slow network performance for the brief duration of time when you are encrypting or decrypting data.

Nowadays, this argument barely holds. We have devices that are built to perform at very high speeds. These devices can handle encryptions without much interference to the network. You might never even notice the network lagging. This is because processors have improved dramatically over the years. You can do so much with very little power in modern times.

Most of the processors we use for computers today are built using AES NI technology. AES NI technology empowers the machines with superior speeds, allowing you to decrypt and encrypt data without a hitch. This technology is reported to enable encryption at three times the usual rate, while it also speeds up the speed of decryption up to ten times.

Implementation Challenges

Implementing encryption is not as difficult as some people imagine it to be. In fact, the most basic form of encryption, SSL certificates, which allow you to browse the internet, actually operate without your knowledge. SSL certificates ensure that the data you access online is protected as you exchange data packets between the browser and your device.

A lot of people still have the notion that you need an expert to install an SSL certificate in your server. This is one of the biggest fallacies as far as encryption is concerned. SSL providers have very simple instructions that you can follow to encrypt your server in a few clicks.

Encryption Is Very Expensive

The issue of affordability is another one that comes down to relative measure. What is expensive for one person might be a drop in the ocean for another. In terms of encryption, a lot of businesses make the wrong assumption that encryption is not affordable, yet you can always enjoy amazing discount offers from different encryption services.

Each encryption program is designed with specific target

audiences in mind. Indeed, some of them might be out of reach for you, but not all of them are. You should do some research to find one that meets your needs. This also allows you to test different experiences, and perhaps as you appreciate the services you receive, you might soon see the need to pay more to access the best encryption services in the future.

Encryption Bulletproofs Your System

While encryption will make it nearly impossible for someone to interpret your information in the wire or air, it does not mean you are entirely safe. Theoretically, cracking cryptographic keys might be difficult, but it's certainly not impossible. There are labs around the world that have dedicated their time and resources to find a way around encryption protocols.

Security breaches still happen, even with some of the best encryption procedures in place. One of the reasons behind this is not that hackers managed to decrypt information, but there is poor handling of encryption keys. Some people store their encryption keys in the same systems that they encrypt. You must exercise due diligence when dealing with encryption keys and protocols so that everything you work on is protected.

Encryption Is for Compliant Organizations

It is amazing the lengths to which people will go to avoid encrypting their data, yet it is their resources that are on the line. Of course, any entity that operates in a regulated market must follow the set guidelines, or they will lose their license to operate. Data security is serious, and authorities are taking a firm stand on it. Companies must exercise due diligence to protect their customers.

Whether you are obligated to encrypt your data or not, it is a logical concept to encrypt sensitive data, as it may fall into the wrong hands, resulting in you fighting legal battles that might run your company into the ground.

The SSL Encryption Myth

SSL is an encryption method that protects your data when browsing online. Given that it almost always just works without any input from your end, many people assume that it encrypts all the data. This is not true. SSL only encrypts data that is being transferred. It does not protect static data. You should take the initiative and encrypt all the data you have access to, especially since it is written on the disk. SSL has been replaced by TLS or Transport Layer Security protocol.

Encrypted Data Cannot Be Stolen

You must realize that there is no security program or project that can offer you 100 percent protection, as mentioned earlier. The best security products in the market will try to offer the top protection to the best of their knowledge. However, a lot of factors come into play that could make it difficult for these programs to protect your data accordingly.

The safest companies and individuals are those who believe that their data is never safe, and as a result, they keep looking for ways of protecting their data. If you believe your data is protected by virtue of the fact that you encrypted it, you become a sitting duck and might only realize your mistake once your data is wiped clean or the FBI is at your doorstep, accusing you of a crime you have no idea about. All of this happens more often that you would believe.

Chapter 4: Preventing Cyber Attacks

In September 2014, Home Depot announced that it was hacked, probably during the spring of that year; this hack led to the theft of the credit card information of 56 million customers. The hack began when malware masquerading as antivirus software infected the POS systems of the company's stores. The company had to pay nearly twenty million dollars in damages and identity theft protection services to those whose information had been compromised.

In February 2015, the largest security breach in healthcare history occurred when a group of cyber criminals, allegedly sponsored by a foreign government, hacked into the Anthem Health Insurance website. The attack led to millions of names, addresses, dates of birth, and the personal health information of individuals insured by Anthem to become compromised. The breach began when an Anthem employee opened up a phishing email; that one email led to well over one hundred million dollars in damages.

In the fall of 2016, while Yahoo was in negotiations to sell itself to the company Verizon, it disclosed that back in 2014, it had been hacked. 500 million email addresses, real names, dates of birth, and other sensitive information that can lead to identity theft had all been hacked. In the early winter of 2016, it disclosed that it had also been similarly hacked back in 2013. This security breach led to compromising the information of one billion users. Yahoo lost $350 million in its sell price to Verizon, as well as its good name. There have been many more, many of which have not been in the news, since then.

The above information isn't intended to scare you. It's intended to sober you into understanding the importance of cybersecurity and protecting yourself online. You may be thinking that these are major companies, so of course, they will be targeted by hackers. But consider this: companies like Yahoo and Target spend millions and millions of dollars every year in cybersecurity yet were still susceptible to security breaches by hackers.

Cybersecurity defends computers, programs and data against hard drive crashes, hackers, viruses, direct attacks and other situations that interrupt or destroy the flow of computer work and safety. Companies, organizations and government agencies receive and process volumes of confidential information, then store and transmit that data to other computers. Ever-increasing cyber-attacks at even the highest levels (The Pentagon, e.g.) demonstrate the need for the development of cybersecurity plans to ensure business flow, protect personal confidentiality and safeguard national security.

Basic measures of protection include maintaining strong authentication practices (passwords, etc.) and not storing sensitive data where it is openly accessible, but a strong cybersecurity plan must also take into account that the digital world expands continually. The cloud, the use of personal devices at work, the growing internet of things (IoT, the inter-connection of home appliances, autos, digital devices, power plants and more)—all of these have created a need to keep up with progress, or even stay a step ahead of it.

The following areas of cybersecurity are key to the development of a strong strategy of protection. These aren't the only vectors you need to be aware of, however, and the first line of defense against cybersecurity threats should always be a healthy dose of caution and common sense.

Critical infrastructure: Essential social services like

electricity, water, traffic lights and medical facilities, when plugged into the Internet, become vulnerable to cyber-attacks. Those in responsible positions must detect, define and protect the weak points while everyone else should consider the effect an attack on the infrastructure would have on them and plan accordingly.

Network security: To protect against damaging intrusions—from both internal and external forces—it is often necessary to require extra log-ins or other measures which are not always completely effective and can also impact productivity. The data generated by these procedures presents another danger, that of missing critical alerts sometimes 'lost in the crowd' of data. Personnel are increasingly seeking ways to incorporate machine learning into the security process in hopes of making the process less susceptible to outside interference of any kind.

Cloud security: As cloud usage proliferates, new challenges to security do the same as each cloud storage system offers virtually unlimited potential for a security nightmare should even one bit of data end up where it is not supposed to be. Statistics show that weekly occurrences of cloud breaches occur on a higher than expected, and far higher than reported, basis, throwing shade on the sense of security that many users feel with the cloud. While new tools to protect are constantly being developed, it is important to note that due diligence remains vital to security.

Application security (AppSec): Although AppSec is the weakest technical point of attack, few entities have paid sufficient attention to the main web vulnerabilities. The first point of AppSec is secure coding. Penetration testing, which is ethical hacking conducted to pinpoint weak spots, is another essential element here.

Internet of things (IoT) security: This category includes items such as printers, appliances, sensors and other critical or noncritical cyber systems that generally lack security protections and can post a threat to the user and those connected to the user. IoT Is a huge vulnerability for home (Residential) networks.

The above categories may seem a bit obscure or overly technical for many readers; to simplify, following is a list of specific actions that can be taken to protect computers:

- Regular reviews of code and testing of units.

- A system designed so that at least two subsystems must be disrupted in order to compromise data and flow.

- Audits of system activity that locate breaches, and off-site storage of the audit trails.

- Security architecture, which defines risks that specific scenarios involve and how and when to apply security controls; this includes standardization of controls according to finance, legal issues etc. how the varying parts depend on each other.

- Coding and user controls can safeguard files and data.

- The most common prevention system for networks are firewalls which can be hardware- or software-based and, if designed appropriately, block unwanted access and some attacks.

- Products that detect in-progress attacks provide follow-up analysis.

Use of a vulnerability scanner that looks for and defines weak spots such as insecure software, vulnerability to malware and open ports.

- Outside auditors can be hired to conduct penetrations tests which find and define vulnerabilities in a system.

- Cryptography can be extremely effective if properly created since it involves input from a key or information that is stolen or other extra input.

- Requiring two factor authentications (use of a password or PIN plus an item such as a card, cellphone or other equipment) is an excellent way to reduce unwanted access to a system or computer.

- Social engineering (physical attack) requires high-level training and even with that, some sensitive military and other government installations have been hacked.

- Attention to backing up and keeping systems up to date with security patches is essential to reducing an attacker's chances of success; also, hiring professional and highly rated security personnel is vital.

- Hardware protection includes the use of USB keys (or dongles) that tunnels between the software application and the key, providing an extra level of protection since the dongle must be hacked. USB dongles can also lock or unlock a computer.

- Microprocessors, or computers-on-a-chip, used with specific software verify the authenticity of hardware and prevent unauthorized access.

It is possible to encrypt hard drives with drive locks to make them inaccessible to malicious intruders. External drives can also be encrypted.

- Capabilities built into cellphones—including Bluetooth, near field communication on non-iOS devices and increased use of thumb print readers and other biometric readers—offer convenient control systems for building access, etc.

- Access control lists (ACLs) are used to confine programs to certain users but have been relatively ineffective since the host computer sometimes allows file access when it should be restricted.

- Regular training and education on security best practices have been shown to be a mitigating influence on solid end user network security habits.

Antivirus software: While the specific details will vary between services, all types of antivirus software are going to scan files as well as the memory usage of your computer to seek out patterns that appear to indicate a high likelihood of malicious use by software known as malware. These days, most antivirus or antimalware programs are a service instead of a single purchase, and in return for either a monthly or yearly fee, they provide you with the latest and greatest when it comes to up to the minute updates regarding new potential threats to your cybersecurity.

While most antivirus software these days actively protects you from potential threats as you encounter them online, it is still a good idea to scan your entire computer periodically, just to make sure that something didn't slip through at an earlier point and time that has since been identified. Most programs will allow you to set up an automatic time each week to scan specific directories or files in real time and will also allow you to schedule prompts for more complete, deep scans.

While installing antivirus software is one of the easiest and most effective ways to protect your computer from malware, it is going to have its limits. The biggest of these is that it can only protect against known threats which means you are still not going to want to venture into the wilds of the internet without care to what sites you are visiting. It is also extremely important to update them regularly for the best results.

Firewalls: Firewalls are extremely useful when it comes to protecting your computer and network from outside attacks from malicious or unnecessary network traffic. It also blocks malicious software from accessing your network. Firewalls can also be configured to block data from various locations or applications while at the same time allowing whitelisted data through.

There are two different types of firewalls, hardware, and software, that control different types of activities and are located in different places. Hardware firewalls, also known as network firewalls are external devices that you physically place your computer and your modem, router, or other network connection. Many internet service providers offer routers with this type of security already built in. This type of firewall is especially useful if you are in the market to protect multiple computers at once and control the various types of activity that pass through them. The biggest advantage of this type of firewall is that it is a completely separate device which means it has its own operating system that the malware would need to crack before it can move on to your primary system.

One of the biggest benefits of software firewalls, on the other hand, is the fact that practically every operating system you can name includes a firewall feature that can be enabled, for free. As such, even if you install a physical firewall you will still want to configure your software firewall as well. Software firewalls are also useful in that they have the ability to control the access that individual processes on the computer have to the network. While running a software firewall is better than nothing, it is important to keep in mind the inherent limitations that come about when the firewall tries to enforce protections on a system that it is a part of. This is going to be doubly true if you are installing a new software firewall onto a system that is already compromised.

When it comes to setting up a firewall successfully, it is especially important to ensure you configure the settings properly. Generally speaking, commercially available firewalls of both varieties come with preconfigured settings that are easy to use. As your needs may be different than the norm, however, it is still important to read any available documentation to ensure that you are getting the most protection possible.

While an effective firewall is going to work to block some attacks, it is important to not use it as an excuse to make poor decisions when browsing online. As with any other type of security, a firewall is only one piece of the puzzle. They primarily serve to protect against traffic with malicious intent, they are not designed to detect malware, which is why it is important it works in tandem with a virus protection software, not as an alternative to it.

Understanding website certificates: If a website is going to operate securely, it needs to obtain what is known as either a host or a site certificate. If a website is asking for your personal information, then checking its website certificates are a good way to determine if it is on the level. If you can't find the certificates for a specific site, and they are asking for your personal information, run the other way and don't look back. Generally speaking, there are two main elements to look for in order to verify that a website is using the proper level of encryption.

First, you are going to want to keep an eye out for the picture of a small, closed padlock, that, depending on your browser, could be found at either the top or the bottom of the browser window. From there, you are also going to want to verify that the website's URL starts with https as opposed to http. By always taking the extra step of looking for these details, you can help protect yourself against attackers and ensure that you know where your information is going before you submit anything.

Assuming the website you are on has a valid certificate, this means that the owner of the site has already taken the steps to verify their site and its security processes, a good sign that it is on the level. When you visit a secure website, your browser will automatically check the website's certificate to ensure it matches with the URL details and that the certificate is signed by an authority your browser recognizes as trusted.

The amount of trust that you can put into a given certificate should be directly proportional to how much you trust the organization in question along with the certifying authority. If the web address is the same as the URL on the certificate, the certificate is signed by a trusted authority, and the date is valid, you can generally be fairly confident that the site you are visiting is on the level. The only way you will ever be able to tell that a website is on the level beyond a shadow of a doubt is by calling the verifying authority directly, which means at some point you will have to exercise a little bit of trust if you want to get anything done online.

If the browser finds a problem during this process, you may be presented with a dialog box indicating an error with the site certificate in question. If you are unsure if a given certificate is valid, it is important to err on the side of caution and not provide that site with any of your personal information. Even if the information you are submitting is successfully encrypted, it is important to still have a clear idea of the company's privacy policy so that you understand what your information is going to be used for before you agree to anything.

Chapter 5: The Future of Cyber Security

Most can agree that hearing about or seeing data breaches on the news is overwhelming. In 2017, one of the largest data breaches occurred, and the victim was the popular credit reporting agency, Equifax. This breach resulted in an estimated 145 million people having their confidential information exposed.

Cybercriminals are constantly adapting and evolving their skills to get around new security measures. It has created a never-ending game where cybersecurity experts continuously develop new and improved security measures that hackers have not figured out how to break into. Once the hackers have figured out how to bypass all the security features, it is up to the experts to create more barriers to protect user information.

In order for cybersecurity to be implemented successfully, it must be improved further until it is capable of handling greater quantities of data. Gil Shwed, co-founder and CEO of Check Point Software Technologies Ltd. told Forbes Magazine that: **"The future of cybersecurity is tightly connected to the future of information technology."**

He believes that in 10 years from now, most of our systems will be associated and driven by computers.

Shwed also believes that not being able to tell who the enemies are in cyberspace and what 'weapons' they are using to attack is an obstacle we must overcome. Anyone who is connected to a network is available all around the world. In addition having an unidentified attacker, most cyberattacks are carried out independently by bots, which seek out the quickest and easiest way to breach a system. This makes everyone who is connected a target to hackers.

Shwed states that to make our defense systems more sophisticated, we must first need to: **"Interconnect our defense systems to act in real time."** Another step we need to make is to rely more on artificial intelligence to help with decision making when dealing with copious amounts of data. Schwed expressed that future cyber experts should be given adequate support as they will form the backbone of an effective defense against sophisticated cyberattacks which will likely increase as technology is further improved. Finally, we need to be able to shield and protect our digital infrastructure. First and foremost, this responsibility falls on our governments to make sure that the harmonious operation of a modern society will not be disrupted. Aside from them, prominent business entities must also be capable of protecting themselves from cyberattacks as many consumers most likely rely on their services. With these two bodies working in conjunction, we might see an effective defense screen that the public will find dependable. After all, if we do not have an all-encompassing defense system, it only takes a single breach to compromise everything.

In ten years, the public will be aware of their digital security as much as their physical security. When they lock their doors at night to keep themselves safe from outsider intruders, the same should be done with their network and computer devices (Schwed, 2017).

The Department of Homeland Security initiated the 'Stop. Think. Connect' campaign which is directed at raising the American public awareness of cybersecurity and urges users to be safer and more secure online. Cybersecurity is not the job of one individual, but instead, is a shared responsibility amongst

51

all people connected to a network or the World Wide Web.

Many people expect that the cybersecurity industry will be worth a trillion dollars by the year 2020. Carl Herberger, VP of

security at Radware had this to say about the future of

cybersecurity:

"The top challenge for cybersecurity isn't preventing data breaches, stamping out ransomware, or preventing ever-more-massive DDoS attacks, it is securing our digital privacy. 2017 and the years to come will dictate the future of cybersecurity, and most importantly, human privacy. Digital threats have evolved quickly and can wreak havoc on our lives, endangering our personal privacy and the privacy of those around us. To tackle this important issue, we need the national government to take a stance on what our digital privacy is. Is it an immutable human right? If so, there needs to be explicit legislation that goes beyond what is currently in place. It needs to protect each and every citizen and hold those who might put our privacy in jeopardy accountable for their actions. This will be the most important cybersecurity decision in the next year, and it will shape the security landscape for years to come"

— Hastreiter, 2018

Top technology innovators believe that, in the future, anything that can be connected to the internet will be connected. In 2015, there were 4.9 million devices connected to the internet. This number increased from millions to billions in just a single year. By 2016, that number had grown from 4.9 million to 3.9 billion (Symantec Corporation).

In the future, it is expected that more cities will become 'smart cities.' The IoT (Internet of Things)

Agenda defines smart cities as:

"A municipality that uses information and communication technologies to increase operational efficiency, share information with the public, and improve both the quality of government services and citizen welfare."

A smart city's main function is to enhance the living conditions of its residents as well as effectively managing its economic growth. This is expected to be done using smart technology and data analysis (Rouse & Shea, 2017).

The future of the internet and cybersecurity is one with a positive outlook that will benefit many and create millions of job opportunities for those people who can understand how computers and networks work. There is no end to cybersecurity evolution in sight for the foreseeable future. Every day, new tactics and security measures are being developed to halt hackers and cybercriminals and help protect individual's sensitive information.

How to Protect Your Business

You need to implement a good security plan and some strategies that will help you secure your platform and protect your interests. In light of the adoption of the GDPR, a lot of companies are making changes to their operations. (Perhaps the threat of heavy fines might be working after all.) One of the benefits of the GDPR is that it allows the average consumer to take back control over their data and how it can be accessed. With this in mind, customers can also report whenever they feel the company is not doing enough to protect their data. To ensure you do not find yourself on the wrong side of the law, we have included a few guidelines that can help you protect your networks and prevent a cyber attack.

Threat Identification

Make it a habit of reporting any threat to your system. Something as simple as unauthorized access might not mean much to you until it is too late. Nothing is ever too small to report when it comes to cyber security. The subsequent loss of information or denial of access to important services is proof of this.

These days, a lot of companies handle information that is very sensitive. This is information that would attract most hackers, especially when they realize your systems use weak security protocols. Remember that hackers are always trawling the internet looking for vulnerabilities that they can exploit. You should not allow them this opportunity.

If someone is going to hack you, at least make their life difficult while attempting it. Take the appropriate precautionary measures to keep the important information about your company safe. Identify and report threats as soon as they happen so that the relevant parties and authorities can look into them and clear your conscience about them before things get out of hand and you lose everything.

Expect an Attack

In the digital world today, it is prudent to expect that an attack is always imminent. This way, you will go about your operations expecting an attack at any given time. With this in mind, the business operations will be carried out with all checks and balances in place.

Try to determine the kind of information you handle and classify those that might be extremely important to hackers from those that are not. Hackers might come after your company for any kind of information. Some might camp in your systems hoping to find a leeway into another company's systems, especially if you deal with other large corporations as third parties.

Astute risk assessment processes will help you make sure you have the right solutions for your problems as soon as they arise. You might not be sure about the type of information you handle, which might be alluring for hackers, so the best way is to make sure everything is protected.

Employee Management

No one has the best insight into your business like your employees do. They are the people who keep your business running and alive. It is only fair that you keep them happy and motivated to work towards the same goals your business has.

In the digital era, loyalty is hard to come by. Your desire to have employees who will do all they can to protect the sanctity of your organization might not be achievable. However, you can take steps to ensure that you never have to risk being shot in the foot by the people you trust. A motivated workforce is always a good thing.

Other than motivating the employees, try to ensure they are aware of their roles in the organization and about the data protection that's required by law. Ensure everyone understands their responsibility and the limit of their liability for the data they handle or protect. Some people freely give away information at times inadvertently, because they are not aware of the risks involved or of the legal ramifications of their actions. Properly educating employees on their legal responsibilities can save you in the long run.

Try to foster an environment where people take responsibility for their actions. This encourages employees to be honest and realize that they're in control of something. They are caregivers and protectors of something important. That being said, you must also take precautionary measures by installing an additional layer of security beyond what you expect employees to do on their part. Your employees might not always be working towards the same goals as you. Where possible, use a password manager to make sure everyone is using an appropriate password.

Two-Factor Authentication (Multi-factor authentication)

Everyone is using it, so why not implement it for your company? You may have noticed that most of the applications you use have switched to two-factor authentication. From Facebook to Gmail, everyone is adding an extra layer of protection for your data. Try to do the same for your company.

Two-factor authentication helps to secure your systems and data by adding an additional verification step to access accounts. Encourage all your employees to use it. Once you enter the password, you receive a message on your phone, without which you cannot access the accounts. This makes it difficult for attackers to go after your system, forcing them to find an alternate way to do so.

While you might not be able to stop hackers from trying to attack your systems, you can do your best to dissuade them altogether. Making the access process as inconvenient and difficult as possible is one of the best ways of achieving this.

System Audits

When was the last time you conducted a system audit on your network? Are you certain about the health status of your network? You need an in-house audit and an external audit to make sure your system is not compromised.

Via a thorough audit, you can learn so much about your vulnerabilities you are exposed to. An external system auditor will also advise you on your current state of affairs in light of industry regulations, so that you can improve your systems and operate a compliant business.

When you start your company as a small firm, things like system audits barely make sense to you, and it seems like you're just spending money that you don't have. You might even consider it once in a very long time. However, as the business grows, you will get a the point where the need for a system audit becomes mandatory. An audit helps you reduce the risks of being hacked. There are so many experts in the industry who can assist you with a system audit, including people who have been in the cyber security industry for many years. Their understanding of cyber security will work to your advantage and help you protect your business.

Signing Off Policies

If you issue mobile devices, tablets, and laptops to your employees, ensure they sign them off before they leave the company. This is important so that privileged information is not leaked. You must also look into encryption protocols for any information that is passed through your networks and devices. The idea here is to maintain confidentiality and integrity.

Insurance Policy

It is prudent in this digital age to have insurance against cyberattacks. Hackers are all over the place, and considering the nature of data and information you process, it's strongly advised that you find an insurance policy that suits your operation. When discussing the risks involved with your insurer, you can learn a lot about the challenge ahead and take that as an incentive to address the possible risk scenarios. An insurance policy will cover your business in the event of a cyberattack. However, by taking the initiative to improve your security based on the risks discussed, you will save yourself from a lot of unnecessary challenges.

Cyberattack Resilience

The nature of risks you are exposed to once your business is connected to the internet is tremendous. Hackers can have extremely detrimental effects on your operations. A lot of companies today depend on the internet, social networks, and technology to remain competitive in their industries. You need to make sure your company is cyber resilient, so you can avoid risks associated with business downtime, revenue loss, and many other costs you might not be aware of as yet.

The size of your company does not matter. Anyone can be a victim of a cyber attack. Taking preventative measures to protect your business will help you gain an advantage in terms of securing your business by reducing your risk exposure. Besides, an astute security profile will also work in your favor, helping you improve your brand image and business reputation, and it can improve your appeal to investors.

Software Updates

One of the simplest ways of protecting your business from attacks is making sure you use updated software. Tech giant HP revealed that applying a software patch at the right time can prevent at least 85 percent of targeted cyber hacks. Software developers often release patches for their programs as frequently as necessary, and more often in response to prevailing cyber threats in the global business world. With this in mind, make sure you get the latest update of whatever software you are using. Regular updates keep your systems protected from vulnerabilities. That is why developers release updates from time to time.

It is shocking how many users do not keep their host OS patched and up do date. Many of these issues are related to small and medium sized businesses that are over worked and understaffed and do not have an IT department, in addition to regular home computers and hosts. Since small and medium businesses comprise a HUGE segment of American business, you can see how this is a ripe goldmine for hackers seeking weaknesses un unpatched operating systems. Not just American, but globally.

Penetration Testing

Not all hackers are bad people. Some hackers are good for your business. To ensure you run a technologically healthy and sound business, you should consider hiring an expert to perform penetration testing and assess the vulnerability of your systems. This is something you should do regularly. You can do it monthly, quarterly, or even annually, depending on what works best for you. The results of these tests will help you identify where your weaknesses lie, and the consultant will also advise you on how to deal with them.

The Need for Proper Training

If you have the best and most secure system in the world but your employees are unaware of how to manage it, you serve no purpose. Training is important to protect your businesses. Most employees unknowingly welcome hackers into your world. They lack the basic understanding of security policies and practices, and how to avoid attacks.

Many companies have their employees signing into computers at cyber cafes with their official business accounts, and at the same time, they forget to sign out and erase their browsing history when they're done.

Other than training your employees, you must also remind them frequently about the policies they have learned and how to enforce them. Ensure everyone adheres to the set guidelines or your employees will be your weakest link, as they always are. Alongside training, make sure everyone learns the importance of taking responsibility for their actions. Employees must protect their departments and dockets. Data access is a critical aspect today that should not be taken lightly. Once everyone understands their responsibilities and accountability for devices in their care, you will have an easier time mitigating cyber hacks.

Protect Your Emails

Among other attacks, phishing attacks are mostly propagated through emails. This is an elaborate form of social engineering where the hackers convince the recipient that they are someone they should trust. Considering that emails are the primary form of communication at the moment, there are many risks involved in using unprotected emails. To protect your emails, you should invest in an anti-spam service that screens your company emails.

Virtual Private Networks (VPN)

It's advised that you purchase VPN software/vendor service and ensure all employees install it on their desktop and mobile devices. If they need to access the company services and they are not within the premises, they must first connect the VPN. VPNs **encrypt** all information that is exchanged through them, improving your security. With a policy like this, all communication takes place over an encrypted channel. Some organizations even run VPN services at work, making it difficult for anyone to breach their systems. VPN's are NOT firewalls, they just encrypt data, but if a device has been compromised, at root level, then your encryption of any data on that machine or sent over the Internet is at risk.

Disaster Management Plan

Make sure you have a solid disaster management plan in place. In the event of a data breach, you should have a recovery plan that will restore your business to full operation in no time while you try to solve the issues behind the scenes. A disaster management plan is not a one-off thing. The plan must be tested periodically and updated to meet the current business demands and highlight resilience to present cyber attack risks.

Privileged User Access

Everyone at your company cannot have the same level of access. Some people only need limited access to enable them to carry out their operations. This especially applies to data access. Some elements of the data in your possession should be restricted to employees with high privilege access.

In data management, you must make sure you have the right controls so that everyone has unique administrative abilities over the data systems your business runs. Sensitive information should only be accessible to very few people in the business.

Another challenge that you will experience is the proper management of removable media. These are the easiest ways for most cyber threats to breach your system. Someone walks in with a USB drive and plugs it into their work computer, hoping to copy their favorite playlist for work. However, the USB drive is infected, and just like that, their computer also is. The infection will soon spread and before you know it, if this was a targeted attack, your business is under siege.

Insist on scanning removable media before it's used in your network; or alternatively, ban them altogether. Encourage users to share information across networks. Networks have firewalls in place that can prevent the transfer or sharing of compromised files. Today most companies have very fast internet access in their offices. Even at home, most people are connected to reliable internet services. You can share gigabytes of data in a very short time. Instead of copying the file, upload it to a cloud storage facility, and share the link for the user to access it at their own time. This does not just save you from waiting for the file to download, but it also saves you on space.

DDoS Protection (Distributed Denial of Service)

DDoS attacks are often targeted attacks. The hackers program a network of computers to direct excess traffic to your website or business. This flood overpowers your network resources, preventing your users from accessing your services. You might also have to pull down your network while you try to solve the problem. These days, there are several prevention mechanisms you can use to protect your business from DDoS attacks.

Gateway Layer Protection

One of the weakest elements in any network is the access point to which your business is connected to the internet. This is the gateway layer. Most attacks are perpetuated through the gateway layer. A lot of them pass by undetected, and you only realize them when your system is hijacked. Update your security apparatus, and make sure you have antivirus programs that can filter web content and protect the gateway layer.

Personal Devices

Encourage employees to avoid bringing their personal devices to work. Personal devices might not have the same security protection as the official work devices do. Leave them at home, and at the same time, do not sign into company accounts on your personal devices. Depending on the nature of your business, it is advisable to issue specific devices to your employees that they can only use at work.

Additional Protection for Critical Operations

All aspects of your business do not hold the same weight. Some are more important than others. Most security breaches target critical information about your business. These are the bits of information upon which the foundation of your business is built. It is wise to provide a higher level of security for this kind of data. Whatever security you use for every other aspect of your business, you should take it a notch higher for the critical elements. Encrypt your communications and data transfers concerning these operations.

State of the Business Address

Remember how the president gives the state of the nation address, updating audiences about the current state the country is in? You should do the same for your business. You might not need to speak to an audience the size of the president's but make sure you inform the relevant parties of the state of the business. How do you do this?

First, you must make sure you have protocols and procedures in place that will guide your operations and ensure that all employees are aware. Review your operations, possible threats, and improve your protection. Make sure that employees are aware of any intrusion detection methods in place so they are confident in the robust nature of their employer. When employees are fully aware of how secure the system is, they will often be taken aback when they notice something fishy, reporting it immediately. This way, everyone in the system is vigilant.

Conduct a mock drill from time to time to evaluate how resilient your protection is. These drills will also help you understand how your employees respond to crisis situations, and you can use that as a necessity for further training. You want the entire workforce ready and able to contain a breach in the unlikely event that you are attacked. Without this, they might make the situation worse.

Endpoint Protection

One of the biggest challenges most businesses struggle with is protecting endpoint access points - in this case laptops and PCs. These devices are vulnerable to attacks, because the employees are not careful about their personal security. Most employees take security measures for granted. Encourage all employees to protect their devices and keep them updated.

Make Cyber Security Everyone's Business

You cannot protect the company on your own. Securing the fortress should be everyone's job. Work with the relevant parties to institute holistic measures regarding cyber resilience. Ensure everyone is aware of their role in protecting the company and their accountability in lieu of their roles.

One of the easiest ways of doing this is by passing a policy stating that everyone must create a strong password, complete with examples of strong passwords. Other than that, insist that passwords must be changed frequently. Assess your employees, procedures, and processes frequently to make sure that your security protocols are up to date and current in light of the pertinent risks you are exposed to.

Chapter 6: Careers in Cybersecurity

Cybersecurity job postings increased nearly 75 percent between 2012 and 2017 and, regardless of what type of career you are interested in pursuing, the job prospects are excellent across the board. What follows are some of the different job options that those in the cybersecurity industry are currently looking to explore. What follows are some of the most popular options on the market today.

Security consultant: A security consultant in the information technology industry is a sort of all-around advisor, guide and security guru. Experts in this role tend to be in charge of designing and implementing the ultimate security solutions based on the threats and needs of a given company which means their day to day tasks will vary substantially. A Security consultant might spend one day determining the most efficient ways to protect a given network, and the next to perform vulnerability testing or risk analyses on another depending on the terms of their individual contracts.

Chief Information Security Officer: As the name implies, the chief information security officer is in charge of all of the security initiatives that a given company puts forth. While these types of professionals were traditionally seen as security enforcers, these days they are more often seen as strategists that help the enterprise avoid cybercrime. They typically appoint and manage a team of other security experts and thus create a strategic plan for the development of information security technologies as well as create security policies for their companies and monitor known security vulnerabilities.

Security Engineer: Security engineer is an intermediate

level job that is typically tasked with things like maintaining and building solutions for a company, often at the behest of the Chief Information Security Officer. These individuals also help to develop new security for an organization's projects and systems and also handle the technical problems the company might face as they arise. They are also often typically responsible for this like installing and configuring firewalls and other types of intrusion detection systems, testing for vulnerabilities and writing automation scripts.

Security Architect: A security architect is often a senior level position that involves designing, overseeing and building the computer and network security for a company, often from the ground up. As such, security architect mush design, research and plan the overarching architecture for all IT projects, perform initial security assessments, create requirements for various networks, firewalls, routers and other network devices.

Incident responder: An incident responder, also known as a computer security incident response team engineer, also known as an intrusion analyst, is essentially the boots on the ground for a company, rapidly addressing threats to security as they come in, in real time. The first responders of the cybersecurity world, their job is to find the cause of an unexpected problem and do anything and everything in their power to ensure that it never happens again. Intrusion analysts also actively monitor systems for potential weaknesses, perform analysis and establish communication protocols both within the company and with law enforcement when an incident occurs.

Computer forensics expert: A computer forensics expert is a type of cybersecurity detective whose job is to analyze and assess evidence from various network devices. Day-to-day this role typically involves conducting investigations, examining data and compiling evidence for legal cases as well as advising law enforcement, legal firms and other paying customers about the credibility of the recovered data.

Penetration tester: Also known as ethical hackers, penetration testers are paid to legally hack into an organization's applications, systems, and networks for the purposes of discovering vulnerabilities that can be patched at a later point and time. This job typically involves creating and performing a variety of formal penetration tests, assessing servers, conducting onsite security assessments and also using social engineering to discover flaws in the personnel network of the company as well.

Security analyst: A security analyst actively works to prevent and detect cyberthreats for a company using any means necessary. It involves planning, upgrading security measures and implementing new controls on existing systems. It also involves determining the potential for risk for a company through the use of external and internal security audits, intrusion detecting and other preventative activities. It is also typically the security analyst's job to coordinate the in-house protection with the security provided by third party vendors as well.

Security software developer: These are the individuals responsible for creating the security software that many of the other individuals on this list use on a daily basis. Depending on their position, a security software developer might be responsible for a team of developers working on software creation tools, or they could be working to develop an overall security strategy, or even participate in the lifecycle development of software systems that support software deployment to customers or testing that work for vulnerabilities.

Security auditor: A security auditor is a mid-level individual who is responsible for examining the effectiveness and security of a company's computer systems and their individual security components before issuing a full report on the same along with recommendations on what can be done to improve the results. These professionals lead, execute and plan security audits for a company that also evaluate overall effectiveness, and efficiency, as well as compliance of required corporate security policies or relevant government regulations as the case, may be.

Conclusion

I hope this book was able to help you garner everything you could about Cybersecurity as a concept. From the text, you should have realized the various applications of Cybersecurity, which is not only relevant to the corporate sphere but also in the practical world when it comes to the use of passwords and login credentials. Methods have been given to protect users from the potential compromise of their accounts such as multi-factor password approaches and using different passwords for different accounts.

We have also considered the Internet of Things as the next big problem as it presents numerous opportunities for hackers to infiltrate and cause damage. The text talks about the attack surface in different facilities depending on the mode that the infiltration uses. If the car, home, and security systems are integrated, then the attack surface becomes exponential because there is a high potential for serious damage if a hack is successful. Unfortunately, the dependence on technology is only increasing, and individuals are unwittingly becoming more vulnerable to the dangers, but they are not paying as much attention as needed to the considerable issues. The attack can come in various forms from ransomware, malware, and data manipulation. Data manipulation is when the hacker does not overtly declare their presence, but manipulates the data after discrete infiltration, such that they are able to surveil or change the outcome without the knowledge of the user.

These are some of the most dangerous attacks, as the criminal can inflict a lot of damage on the system for a long period of time without the knowledge of the user—until they decide to make it known. There have been examples which have been given in the text which show espionage and mass scale cyberattacks. Imagine if someone placed a key-logging tool in your personal computer and became privy to your passwords to social media, finances, school, or your organization. It would not take a lot of effort for this individual to ruin your life. There have been various solutions given to decrease your attack surface and mitigate the risks of cyberattacks. These can also be used on a small scale to protect yourself as an individual from such infiltrations.

The next step is placing advanced authentication when it comes to internal collaborators. After all, the goal is to minimize the risk of passwords being hacked—so it would be a good idea to use two-factor authentications. Google presents the perfect example in their security protocols by the way they use two-step verification, where the password has to be backed by a code sent to the user's mobile device.

You also need to authenticate the external collaborators. There are inevitable risks which come with sharing data to the external suppliers, clients, and partners that are essential in business. In this case, you need to know how long the data is being shared for and apply controls to supervise the sharing permissions that can be stopped when required. If not for anything else, it would give you peace of mind to know that the information is safely being handled. The future of cybersecurity lies in setting up frameworks, as individuals and as corporations, to filter the access to information and sharing networks.

To avoid cybercrime from evolving, and to not become better at infiltration and such, cybersecurity needs to stay a practice that adapts to growing problems, thus far, the hackers/attackers are outpacing defenders.